By the same author

UP THE NORAN WATER (Methuen and Co. 1934)
SEA BUCKTHORN (H.T. Macpherson, 1954)
THE PONNAGE POOL (M. Macdonald, 1968)

Collected Poems

Helen B. Cruickshank

PUBLISHED BY
REPROGRAPHIA

23, Livingstone Pl. Edinburgh EH9. 1PD.

●

Illustration and Design by G. Gordon Wright

SBN 903065 02 9

Printed in Scotland by
Econoprint Ltd., Edinburgh

AUTHOR'S NOTE

This collected Edition contains all the poems published in my three previous books, along with such earlier verses that I can now locate. The latter appeared in numerous periodicals, and have not been previously included in book form.

This prentice-work is now printed in the earlier portion of the book.

Towards the end of the book are printed poems written since my retiral from the Civil Service, in which I spent forty years of my professional life.

Since I am now in my eighty-sixth year, and the last surviving member of my family, much of this later work is concerned (not too gloomily I hope) with the problems of identity, and of old age.

I hope readers will agree with me in thinking that my verse in Scots is stronger than my verse in English. I am grateful for my schooling in Angus, which is still a stronghold of the Scots tongue.

H.B.C. 1971

ACKNOWLEDGMENTS

Acknowledgments are given where appropriate to the following publications:

Akros, The Apple, Catalyst, Chambers's Journal, Country Life, Edinburgh Evening Dispatch, Fife and Angus Annual, Gallovidian Annual, Glasgow Evening News, Glasgow Herald, A Glen Anthology, New Age, New Shetlander, New Statesman, Poetry Review, P.O.T.H., Punch, Scots Magazine, Scots Week-end Book, Time and Tide.

CONTENTS

9

BACKGROUND

Frost, I mind, an' snaw,
An' a bairn comin' hame frae the schule
Greetin', nearly, wi' cauld,
But seein', for a' that,
The icicles i' the ditch,
The snaw-ploo's marbled tracks,
An' the print o' the rabbits' feet
At the hole i' the wire.

"Bairn, ye're blue wi' cauld!"
An apron warmed at the fire,
An' frostit fingers rubbed
Till they dirl wi' pain.
Buttered toast an' tea,
The yellow licht o' the lamp,
An' the cat on the clootie rug
Afore the fire.

BEECH LEAVES

Today I leaned on a gate looking into a turnip-field,
And while I was idly comparing
The thin green rows on the ridges of earth
With mustard and cress,
I plucked a glossy new leaf from the old beech-hedge
That ran between the field and the road,
And holding the leaf against my lips
I blew on it, making a noise, half-whistle, half-squeak
Until the leaf was torn.
And with the sound, my mind ran backwards
Fifty years,
And I saw myself, a sturdy lassie of six,
Going to school with my two big brothers
Down the hill to the village, where we were the "gentry-kids"
Among the rough-spoken children there.
(In Jim's class no one else wore a linen collar, and so
His class-mates called him "The Laird").
I remembered the long beech-hedge at one side of the road,
By the wood that no one entered.
On the other side was a ditch and a high green bank
Topped by the fence of a field of corn.
We used to search for sourocks among the grass, and eat them,
And once the boys found a wasps' byke in the bank,
And gathering other boys from the school, attacked it
With switches of broom,
Sending me first, their protesting sister,
Up the road away out of danger;
For I always wanted to do what the boys did,
And did, too.
But this time I felt on the side of the wasps,
For what had they done that their house should be harried and
    torn?
So I went up the road and watched, hoping the boys would
    get stung,
And hoping, too, that they wouldn't.
And I remember how mad we were when Mother said "No,"
When we pled to go barefoot like everyone else in the school.
So we did it.

14

We hid our stockings and shoes under a whin
At the top of the hill,
And padded along in the soft warm dust at the side of the road.
In the afternoon coming home,
We would wash our feet in the ditch, at the splash of the
    "stroop"
Where the water drained out of the high corn-field
(I washing carefully in between my toes
With the sponge that was tied to my slate).
Then we put on our shoes and went home, hoping no one would
    tell
They had seen the three of us barefoot.
Oh! it was lovely, the feel of your toes on the soft warm dust,
And the splash in the ditch, and the long cool grass to lie on.
I liked best the side of the road with the ditch and the bank,
But I liked the hedge side, too, and the wood
That no one ever entered.
We used to pluck the leaves of the beech
When they were glossy and fresh and green,
And blow on them till they whistled and tore,
Just as I did today.
Two men who passed me today on their Sunday walk
Looked strangely at the elderly woman in black
Blowing upon a leaf.
They thought I was mad, I suppose.
They wouldn't know I was living again
The days when I was happy and young,
Before the storms of life had blown
And shaken and torn me.

KEEPIT IN

O, fient a bit o' lear ha'e I,
It beats me hoo X equals Y,
An' nine times nine hooe'er I try
    I canna mind ava, sir.
But I ken whaur the yorline biggs,
An' peewits lay atween the rigs,
An' whaur the brock his burrow digs,
    An' moudiewarps an a', sir.

A squirrel nests in Jerrat's Wood,
An' on the dam an early brood
O' waterhennies has begood
    Amang the reeds tae steer, sir.
But I maun bide inside an' say
My Latin verbs an' trash like thae—
O' dinna keep me in the day,
    Indeed I'm feelin' queer, sir.

The keeper doon at Lowrie Mill,
Is hunting tods on Rossie Hill,
Were I ootside I'd no feel ill
    I ha'ena muckle doobt, sir.
My heid is bizzin' like a bee,
My een are het, I canna see,
Ye waste your time an' tawse on me!
    O, *please*, can I get oot, sir!

BEASTIES

Clok-leddy, clok-leddy
   Flee awa' hame,
Your lum's in a lowe,
   Your bairns in a flame;
Reid-spottit jeckit,
   An' polished black e'e,
Land on my luif, an' bring
   Siller tae me!

Ettercap, ettercap,
   Spinnin' your threid,
Midges for denner, an'
   Flees for your breid;
Sic a mischanter
   Befell a bluebottle,
Silk roond his feet—
   Your hand at his throttle!

Moudiewarp, moudiewarp,
   Howkin' an' scartin',
Tweed winna plaise ye,
   Nor yet the braw tartan,
Silk winna suit ye,
   Naither will cotton,
Naething, my lord, but the
   Velvet ye've gotten.

APRIL, 1918

The blossom's on the blackthorn, the gold is on the whin,
The crimson tufts are on the larch, the birks are veiled in green,
An' bonny 'mang the Angus Braes the Prosen Waters rin —
   But it's oh! for the lad that gaed tae Flanders!

Here alang the Prosen Haughs he used tae tend his sheep,
Risin' in the lambin' time when I was fast asleep;
Far ayont the Angus Braes the tides o' battle sweep —
   And it's oh! for the lad that lies in Flanders!

LIZZIE

Bessie walked oot wi' Tam yestreen,
    Robin is coortin' Mary,
The halflin-laddie is unco keen
    On Kate, doonbye at the dairy;
But naebody comes a-coortin' me—
Me, that's bonnier nor the three!

Bess is a thowless shilpit quean,
    Mary is mim and primsy,
Kate has a tongue as sharp's a preen,
    Forbye, she's muckle an' clumsy.
It's queer, they ha'e a' got lads but me—
Me, that's cleverer nor the three!

Tam, he's lanky and pirny-taed,
    Robin's owre fond o' siller;
As for Kate an' the halflin-lad,
    What can he see intil her?
In fac', it's clear as clear's can be
There's nane o' them guid eneuch for me!

Kate, she leuch i' my face the day,
    An' sneered, the impident hizzie!
"Ye've muckle conceit o' yersel', ye ha'e,
    But ye're green wi' envy, Lizzie!"
Envy? My wumman, juist bide a wee,
I'se warrant I wed the best o' the three!

I'm wastin' mysel' on this weary ferm,
    My thochts tae the toon are turnin',
I'll tak' a place at the Marti'mas term,
    An' be dune wi' milkin' an' kirnin'.
An' Kate will see what she will see,
For mebbe a p'liceman will mairry me!

THE UNIVERSAL AUNT

There was a hen at Tipperty
    That hatched a brood o' ducks,
An led them tae the waterside
    Wi' prood maternal clucks.

And when the fluffy little teds
    Were launched upo' the dam,
A ferly see, in stappit she,
    An' wided whaur they swam.

Her scaly legs grew white as milk,
    Weet were her feather breeks,
An' in she raxed her horny neb
    Whan doon dabbed yellow beaks.

She herded a' her paiddlin' brood
    Frae cressy bank tae bank,
An' wided but an' wided ben
    On carefu', balanced, shank.

"Noo heaven uphaud ye, skeely hen,
    Ye're daft, ye love-a-duck!"
Her beady e'e she winked at me,
    An' "Cluck," she said, juist "Cluck!"

AFTER RAIN

Reluctant sunlight creeps across the hill,
And under its fair progress, genial, slow,
The new-shorn ewes gleam momently like
    snow,
And all the corrie, that was grey until
That heavy, sullen cloud had worked its will,
With colour warm and rich is now aglow,
Crimson the sundews and the sphagnum
    show,
And thyme and heather rocky crannies fill,
O'er sparkling granite rocks, with roar and
    rush,
Down to the falls the amber torrent rides,
Swollen by rain from all the boggy hollows.
The air is sweet with scent of myrtle bush,
Across the glen a noble rainbow strides,
And where the sunburst goes, bright colour
    follows.

THE DUNDEE MILLWORKER'S WIFE

Quit this noisy stoury toun,
　　Wi' its curst machinery;
We will seek the heather broun
　　An' the birches' greenery.

Seeck am I o' shops an' streets,
　　Come, an' lat's be stirrin', O,
Whaur the muirland lambie bleats
　　An' the grouse are whirrin', O.

Bring your cuttie-knife, my chiel',
　　An' the twine for bindin', O,
Heather reenges sell richt weel,
　　Ye will sune be findin', O.

We will tak' the drovers' road,
　　Owre the muir an' heather, O,
Nane to see but sheep an' tod,
　　What we'll mebbe gether, O.

Rabbit stew intil the pan,
　　Speir na whaur we got it, O;
Never lift the lid, my man,
　　Efter it is pottit, O.

Birken twigs tae mak' a bleeze
　　(Wheesht, for roastit chicken, O!),
Guddlit troot, an' gin ye please,
　　Berries for the pickin', O.

First, we'll tak' the road tae Blair,
　　Fiech! this toun sae smoky, O!
Tinklers baith, without a care,
　　Haste, an' fill your pokey, O!

WHEN GLOAMIN' FA'S

When gloamin' fa's on Prosenside,
An' nicht comes stealin' saft an' still,
An' bairns are beddit safe an' soond,
An' Tam's hame frae the mill,
O, then I lo'e tae stand an' gaze
As I wad never ha'e my fill
At stars that prick the darklin' sky
   Abune Kinwherrie Hill.

My man, he dovers owre the fire
Noo a' his stoury wark is dune,
Or tak's the fiddle frae the wa'
An' soothes an auld-warld tune;
But I maun stand ootowre the yett
An' watch the bonny stars abune,
Or steep mysel' intil the licht
   O' siller-sheenin' mune.

"Ye'll tak' your daith o' cauld," says Tam,
"Come on, noo, Jeanie lass, inbye!"
I canna tell him what I feel,
I doobt he'd think me fey;
But peace steals saftly like the nicht
Oot o' the slowly-darklin' sky
Owre a' the cares I thocht I had—
   I canna tell you why.

RAB IN THE FIELD

I haud my ploo and steady guide
Auld Dan an' Whitestar side by side,
An' happit in my he'rt I hide
　　My love for Ceenie Sutherland.

The blackie in yon hawthorn tree,
The whaup that whistles owre the lea,
The jenny-wren sae jimp an' wee,
　　A' sing o' Ceenie Sutherland.

I hear the burnie's wimplin' sang,
It never stops the hale day lang,
Like me, its thochts are ever thrang
　　Wi' bonny Ceenie Sutherland.

My he'rt's a field that's plooed by her,
In every inch I feel a stir,
Her mark's on every rig an' fur,
　　That cuttie, Ceenie Sutherland!

An' when the first green blades are thro'
This fifteen-acre field I ploo,
I'll try my luck, an' find oot hoo
　　I stand wi' Ceenie Sutherland.

TRYSTED

I wandered at the gloamin' time
  Ayont the dyke, abune the wood,
An' watched the frosty evenin' rime
  Steal roun' the ferm-toon like a shroud.
I heard a lassie blithely lilt
  As she gaed clatterin' to the byre,
An' in the searchin' cauld I smelt
  The warm reek o' the kitchen fire.

November nichts are raw an' damp,
  An' dowie mith the plooman be
That kentna o' a cheery lamp
  To swing upon his rafter-tree.
But Love's the lantern burnin' high
  That sune will shine on Jean an' me,
She's singin' as she milks the kye,
  An' faith! but she sings bonnily.
For Jean an' me ha'e trysted troth,
  An' man an' wife at Yule we'll be,
An' I am safe to tak' my oath
  She's singin' while she thinks o' me.

AT THE CROSS ROADS

O, but I wonder
  Whither it goes
Does this road lead me
  To friends or foes?
It calls you, calls you,
Whatever befalls you—
Why do you wonder
  Whither it goes?

I tire of thinking,
  Is this the way?
Surely Beauty
  Will not betray!
Follow then, follow,
By hill and hollow;
You tire of thinking,
  Is this the way?

Claim I Beauty
  As friend and guide,
And daily companion
  By my side.
Choose ye weeping
And troubled sleeping,
To live with Beauty
  As friend and guide?

Such my choice is,
  Right or wrong,
So that Beauty
  Teach me song.
To-day and to-morrow,
You shall have sorrow,
This your choice is,
  Right or wrong.

Beauty shall lead you
  By stormy ways
To strange companions
  All your days:
Dark roads taking,
Strange songs making,
Let her lead me
  By stormy ways!

WILD GEESE

The earth frostbound, an azure sky,
A far-off, unfamiliar cry;
Look! Flashing in the sunlight high
A wondrous sight!
With stretching necks and beating wings
The wedge of tameless, urgent things
Drives thro' the air, and ceaseless sings
In rapid flight.

As swift, as wild, is loveliness,
Whose winged visions wound and bless
The mind that struggles to express
The passing bright.
So, thrilled and shaken by their cry
I saw, far up the echoing sky,
The gaggle of wild geese go by
And pass from sight.

UNREGARDED SONG

I will pick my love a hundred milkworts,
Sprigs of the tiny milkwort, turquoise-blue,
From turfy banks and little heather hummocks
    Noon-warm, or wet with dew.

I will pick my love a hundred milkworts
Building my massy bouquet by degrees,
Fifty today, the rest by noon tomorrow,
    Robbing the early bees.

I will pick my love a hundred milkworts
In crystal air, song-threaded by the wren,
Where conies jink and bob about their warren,
    And cuckoo chimes again.

I will give my love a hundred milkworts,
Her gentle hands will span their rush-tied blue,
Of simple country pleasuring the symbol,
    And say — My dear, for you.

SEPTEMBER NOON

Russet bracken, a spider spinning,
   White tails bobbing in burrows of sand;
A finch is feeding on silver thistle,
   A late bee settles upon my hand.

Still are the woods in the heat of autumn,
   Fearless the rabbits, so still I lie
Happy to see the spider spinning,
   While dreams like down go floating by.

A golden leaf from a yellowing birch-tree
   Softly falls on the spider's thread;
The silken line on the frond is broken
   The coloured finch from the thistle fled.

Stiffly I rise from the bracken covert,
   The rabbits scuttle in panic flight;
The golden moment I held is over,
   The air gone chill, and the sun less bright.

The cares of living come back in legions,
   The glamour is gone from the autumn wood,
So frail a thread as the spider's spinning
   Can carry a dream, or enchant a mood.

THE HARP

(played by Nora Johnstone)

She played on the strings of her Irish harp,
    A queer old Irish air.
It stole on the ears of her listening guests
    Like a sigh from a moorland bare;
And the walls of the room, they melted away,
    And the listeners seemed to be
In a soft green glen, where a brown burn ran
    Through the peat bogs down to the sea.

And over the moorland the westering sun
    Sent slanting golden beams,
And then in the still air rose a sound
    Like the music heard in dreams.
Plaintive, haunting, and far away
    The spiral tune ascended;
With the blue turf-smoke, and the sweet bog scents,
    And the song of the burn all blended.

And an ancient man strode over the hill,
    His bagpipes bravely blowing,
With never a glance to the right or left,
    To see where he was going.
Moleskin breeches, velveteen coat,
    Clay-pipe in his green hat-band,
Fey blue eyes, and streaming grey locks
    Oh! the tune that he piped was grand.

The children flocked to the cabin door
    As the piper came marching along.
They ran at his heels, and they sang and danced,
    But he paid no heed to their song.
Down the green valley he quickly went,
    And still on his pipes did play,
Till the throbbing music that rose and fell
    In the distance died away.

The low hills darkened, the night came on,
    And the piper played no more.

And we woke with a start, in a music-room,
    And the harpist's tune was o'er.

THE FAIRY FOLK

One evening at Midsummertide,
When moths were on the wing,
I heard upon a mountain-side
A tiny tinkling laugh, and spied
A fairy jingaring.

A funny little elf in red,
No bigger than my thumb,
Was perched upon a bracken-head
And on a harp of spider-thread
Right busily did thrum.

And fairy folk, so light, so fleet,
Went dancing round and round.
Their fluttering garments wafted sweet
Faint perfumes as their twinkling feet
Flashed o'er the thymy ground.

And some were dressed in filmy blue
And some in green and white,
And sparkling ornaments of dew
Shone in the hair of one or two
In little points of light.

Enchanted by the fairy folk,
"Bravo!" at last I cried;
But oh! the magic spell I broke—
They vanished like a wisp of smoke
Upon the mountain-side.

And all that I could find of them
Was just this little rhyme,
A web upon a bracken-stem,
A blade that held a dewdrop gem,
And scent of bruisèd thyme.

THE PONNAGE POOL

"... Sing
Some simple silly sang
O' willows or o' mimulus
A river's banks alang."

–HUGH MACDIARMID

I mind o' the Ponnage Pule,
The reid brae risin',
Morphie Lade,
An' the saumon that louped the dam,
A tree i' Martin's Den
Wi' names carved on it;
But I ken na wha I am.

Ane o' the names was mine,
An' still I own it.
Naething it kens
O' a' that mak's up me.
Less I ken o' mysel'
Than the saumon wherefore
It rins up Esk frae the sea.

I am the deep o' the pule,
The fish, the fisher,
The river in spate,
The broon o' the far peat-moss,
The shingle bricht wi' the flooer
O' the yellow mim'lus,
The martin fleein' across.

I mind o' the Ponnage Pule
On a shinin' mornin',
The saumon fishers
Nettin' the bonny brutes—
I' the slithery dark o' the boddom
O' Charon's Coble
Ae day I'll faddom my doobts.

THE GIPSY LASS

The road I traivel's no' for ye,
    Sandy, Sandy,
The weird that's mine ye maunna dree,
    Sandy dear my lad,
Ye maunna link your life wi' shame
Nor think tae tak' intae your hame
A gipsy lass withoot a name,
    Sandy dear my lad.

I never kent wha faithered me,
    Sandy, Sandy,
For mither's gane wi' twa or three,
    Sandy dear my lad.
The gipsy he'rt maun ever range
An' sae it's mebbe no' that strange,
That I, like her, am fond o' change,
    Sandy dear my lad.

I couldna thole a hoose o' stane,
    Sandy, Sandy,
For me, the brackens up the lane,
    Sandy dear my lad.
Your een sae bonny blue an' clear
Wad tine their cheery look, I fear,
Afore we had been wed a year,
    Sandy dear my lad.

An' tho' I lo'e ye weel the noo,
    Sandy, Sandy,
I doobt I'd gi'e ye cause tae rue,
    Sandy dear my lad.
Sae gang your ways. They'll ne'er be mine,
For you an' me that kissed maun twine.
(But oh, I'm wae my lad tae tine,
    Sandy dear my lad).

RONALD MARR

My father was a North man, a stern man, a still man,
  Whose nature was alien to laughter and fun;
His God was a just God, a distant august God,
  And I Ronald Marr, am my father's son.

My mother was a South maid, a merry maid, a gay maid,
  Whose heart longed for laughter, variety and fun.
My father's silence chilled her, my father's gloom killed her,
  And I, Ronald Marr, am my mother's son.

And I am impulsive, reserved, unstable,
  Disciple by turns, of gloom and of fun.
My dual nature snares me, my dual nature tears me,
  For I am my father's and my mother's son.

THE EYEBROW ASKS

One eyebrow's straight, accepting
  The world as it is:
The other rises in an arch
  In a perpetual quiz.

That's how things are. Why worry?
  Says one: the other, Why
Are they like that? I'll challenge
  And fight until I die.

And so the see-saw rises
  And falls perpetually:
The rider on the rocking-horse,
  Hamlet, you or me?

IN GLENSKENNO WOODS

Under an arch o' bramble
  Saftly she goes,
Dark broon een like velvet,
  Cheeks like the rose.

Ae lang branch o' the bramble
  Dips ere she pass,
Tethers wi' thorns the hair
  O' the little lass.

Ripe black fruit, an' blossom
  White on the spray,
Leaves o' russet an' crimson,
  What wad ye say?

What wad ye say to the bairn
  That ye catch her snood,
Haudin' her there i' the hush
  O' Glenskenno Wood?

What wad ye say? The autumn
  O' life draws near.
Still she waits, an' listens,
  But canna hear.

IN JULY

The summer air is sweet with hay,
    The silken oats are shot with red,
The hedgerows that were starred with may
    Bear roses now instead.

The honeysuckle decks the lane,
    And rosebay willow-herb the hill,
And fragrant meadowsweets again
    The grassy ditches fill.

But camp-fire smoke, and bell-tent hood,
    And merry whistling lads from town
By splashing stream or shady wood,
    Are surely summer's crown.

WORDS FOR MUSIC

Down by the willow tree a little bird is singing,
    "Love, lassie, love, while the blossom's on the lea."
All about the meadows green the marigolds were springing,
    Burning in the gloaming as by went she,
Down by the willow tree her hands a maid is wringing.
    "Run, burnie, run, o'er thy stony bed, and me!"
All about her floating hair the waterweeds are clinging.
    "Love, lassie, love!" sings the birdie on the tree.

SLEEP

Like swans upon a jet-black pool
Sleep sailed into my mind,
And softly turned and turned about
Downy and calm and cool;
So soft, so cool, so kind.

And little eddies rippled there
In darkness, and a flute
Played in a distant grove of pine
The Londonderry Air;
And then was mute.

And o'er the dark flute-haunted grove
Arose a star. It shone
A moment silver on the pool,
The dream of one I love; I love,
And then was gone.

ON NOT COUNTING SHEEP

Seven apples trees, a willow and a pine
At the top of the garden, that makes nine.
A privet and a cypress, a winter-flowering cherry,
A birch and a rowan, green tassel, crimson berry.
A juniper, a hazel, a laurel and a gean,
A yellow rose, a plum-tree, with no plums to glean.
I'm counting my trees; no, I'm not counting sheep —

A rowan at the gateway,

I'm —— falling—— asleep.

DEDICATION TO GLENESK

I sing of Prosen
Or of Noranside,
But these are not my dears.
Another stream is running in my blood,
Grown dearer thro' the years:
One loved since childhood
Like a mother's face,
No child can e'er portray;
Too dear, too near,
Too much a part of me,
And now, too far away.

A child cannot describe
His mother's face,
Nor can I paint aright
The loveliness
Inhabiting the place,
The source of my delight.

Maskeldy, Unich,
Waters of the Tarf,
Effock, Cardowan, Lee,
GLENESK
*This book my pilgrimage thro' Life,
I dedicate to thee.

(*"Sea Buckthorn") 15 May 1954

SHY GEORDIE

Up the Noran Water
In by Inglismaddy,
Annie's got a bairnie
That hasna got a daddy.
Some say it's Tammas's
An' some say it's Chay's;
An' naebody expec'it it,
Wi' Annie's quiet ways.

Up the Noran Water
The bonnie little mannie
Is dandled an' cuddled close
By Inglismaddy's Annie.
Wha the bairnie's daddy is
The lassie never says;
But some think it's Tammas's,
An' some think it's Chay's.

Up the Noran Water
The country folk are kind:
An' wha the bairnie's daddy is
They dinna muckle mind.
But oh! the bairn at Annie's breist,
The love in Annie's e'e—
They mak' me wish wi' a' my micht
The lucky lad was me!

IN ANY GLEN

The bracken's creepin'
Whaur the sheep aince fed,
An' whaur the kye, the tansy;
The nettle, hemlock,
An' the docken spread,
Whaur smiled the rose, the pansy.
A staney rickle
Is the ancient hame,
Scarce ony soul can mind it;
Only the sentinel rowan's
Scarlet flame
Will help the seeker find it.

Yet here the clatter
O' the bairnies' feet
Aince set the rafters ringin';
Bess the black collie
Friskin' at the peat,
The nearby burnie singin'.
The hinny bee
Was thrang upon the hill
Whaur growes the bonny heather.
The hinny bee
The stand o' skeps wad fill—
But wha the combs wad gether?

Ay, wha will gether
What oor kintra has
Tae offer them that love her?
The very grouse "Come back,
Back, back, back" ca's
Frae oot her caller cover.
O men, wha stinkin'
Tenements will thole,
Will ye rot there for ever?
Or will ye tak' the spade,
An' no' the dole,
Save Scotland wi' endeavour?

There's work an' weal
For you, an' for your bairns,
Gin ye wad but besteer ye,
Oor nation then be mair
Than burial-cairns.
The remedy lies near ye!

HAMEOWRE SANG FOR ANGUS

Fa keeps me eident weyvin' 'oo
An' nearly wud wi' wark to do
The tub an' hippen-towie fu'?
  My little Angus Doddy, O.

His daddy's far across the sea,
An' fain to dandle him an' me,
But fan, O fan will that day be.
  My little Angus Doddy, O?

His mither's aften sair forfochen
The sacket disna care a docken—
Sae lang's his drouthy mou I slocken—
  My little Angus Doddy, O.

But wheesht, the bairnie's sleepin' noo
Wi' ne'er a canker on his broo,
Nor thocht o' war wi' a' its grue.
  My little Angus Doddy, O.

His faither's far across the sea,
An' fain to dandle him an' me,
And sune, O sune may that day be,
  My little Angus Doddy, O.

Sung to Traditional Air: "My only Jo and Dearie, O,"
in One-Act Scots Play, "The Birken Bush."

41

ONLY DAUGHTER

She mucks the byre
An' slices neeps,
I' the frosty dark
While her father sleeps.
A' green wi' sharn
An' warped wi' weet
Man's buits are on
Her shauchlin' feet.
Wi' hands a' grime
An' gnarled an' roch
She stirs the meat
I' the gussie's troch,
Till frae the door
A girnin' man
Cries 'Whaur's my parritch,
Maggie Ann?''

A couch of down,
A silk bedspread,
A tray of tea
Brought to her bed;
Red slippers for
Her dainty feet,
A maid to wait on
Marguerite.

The hands o' lovely
Lady Jane
Were aince nae safter
Than your ain.

They brushed an' dressed
Her hair sae fine,
But noo they ser'
The gutsy swine.
O, Fate has led ye
A bonny dance
Tae bring ye frae
Your place in France,
Tae toil an' moil
For a weedow-man,
O grey hard-workin'
Maggie Ann!

A WOOIN'

I canna love the new love
For mindin' on the auld.
I canna lat ye woo, love,
Altho' ye are sae bauld.
I canna lat ye kiss me,
Sae dinna come sae near.
Haud aff, noo I'm tellin' ye!
I canna be your dear.

Noo, ye are surely daft, lass,
Tae nurse your loss sae lang;
Noo, dinna be sae saft, lass,
But lat the past gae hang!
O loyalty's a bonny thing,
An' faithfu' folk are fine,
But we are livin' noo, lass,
An' no' lang syne!

I canna love the new love.
He loves eneuch for twa.
I canna lat ye woo, love.
O, I will melt your snaw!
I canna lat ye kiss me—
Hoots, I'll no' wait your will!
My he'rt's a nest will shelter ye,
Lie still, my bird, lie still!

THE AULD WIFE SPEAKS

Lassie, tho' your he'rt be sair
At tynin' o' your dear, O,
Gang intil the caller air,
I trow 'twill bring ye cheer, O,
Look an' lauch at a' ye see
An' aye the twinkle in your e'e
Will drive awa' the tear, O!

Lauchin' een see mony a thing
Wi' vision braw an' clear, O.
Begrutten een a curtain hing
Black an' unco drear, O.
Driech a while the weird ye dree,
But aye the twinkle in your e'e
Will drive awa' the tear, O!

Your jo has left ye? Quit your grief!
He's but a worthless leear, O.
He wasna worth a docken leaf,
Far less a lass's tear, O.
There's better fish still in the sea,
Sae licht the twinkle in your e'e,
An' wile anither dear, O!

COONTIT OOT

Eenerty, feenerty, fickerty, feg,
I saw a man wi a crookity leg,
Irkie, birkie, story, rock,
Airmin a wife wi a raggity frock,
Black pudden, white troot,
Fat were thae twa tinks aboot?
El, del, domin, eg,
She rappt at the door an beguid tae beg,
The collie flew oot and gied her a fleg,
He nippit her ankle, an tore her frock
An, tan, toose, jock,
My man woke up, an threw them oot,
Black pudden, white troot.

An that's the end o my story.

VILLAGE SCENE

Denty Davie, Denty Davie,
Wanderin' mind an' feet,
Lauched an' noddit tae the birds
In the winter wheat.

"Howk for worms aboot the ruit,
Dinna howk the seed,
Wait a whilie, bird-an-joe,
Ye'll get a' ye need.

"Midge an' mite aboot the braird,
Wheat intill the ear!"
Denty Davie stottered on,
Lauchin' lood an' clear.

TREES

The parson's voice droned pious word on word
    I did not hear for sorrow dulled my ears.
I dropped the cord within your grave, and blurred
    Black figures wavered through my smarting tears,
"Oh, I shall faint!" I thought, and on the tree
    That grows beside your grave I put my hand.
My grief the plane-tree seemed to understand,
    So much it comforted and steadied me.

I'm glad you have those trees so near your mound
    (Plane-trees in front of you and pines behind);
For you loved trees. At night-time by the sound
    The wind made in their leaves you knew their kind.
You will not feel so lonely where you lie
    If you can hear the pattering of rain
On smooth broad leaves, and say, "That is a plane,"
    Or, "Surely those are pines that sough and sigh."

Kirriemuir Hill, April, 1924

48

AT BRIDGE OF TILT

If May can trouble still the Dead,
So that they stir, uncomforted,
Regretting all the loveliness
They're cheated of in Death's duress,
I think, tho' they uneasy lie
Where these bright waters hurtle by,
They will find gentle peace again
And balm of Beauty for their pain;
For in this grey-walled lichened place
Is wrought a miracle of grace—
Windsown, between the leaning tombs,
Are drifts of lilac-tinted blooms,
Whose colour lies upon the green,
So lovely, tranquil, and serene,
That strange and subtle solacing
To quick and dead alike they bring.
And tho' the cuckoo calls above
His wayward notes of change and love,
These fragile cuckoo-flow'rs in hosts
Will lull to sleep uneasy ghosts
Who stir, awakened by the cry
Of cuckoo, where the Tilt goes by.

SHOOTING GUEST, NONCONFORMIST

You promised I should see the golden eagle;
Speckled brown adders basking in the sun;
Proud antlered stags and herds of red hinds leaping
Across great rocky corries, rainbow spanned;
Peat mosses where three thousand feet on high
The luscious scarlet averens* are glowing;
Pools where the otter stalks for salmon flesh;
Heron, grey on a green sky, solemn floating.

But these I saw while you to butts were striding
Guided by servile gillies to your sport,
Fast-rooted bracken where the corn once ripened;
Roofless and ruined homesteads by the score;
Once-fertile gardens, mildewed, choked with weed,
Hemlock and nettle where the children played.

*cloudberries

GRANNY

I'm deif, an' canna hear
   The birdies sing,
But fine I ken the unquait
   Lilt o' Spring,
For Rab my grandson shaves
   Noo ilka nicht,
An' daunders, careless-like,
   Oot o' my sicht,
Awa' up Whinny Brae
   An' Roods links he,
An' comes na hame till ten
   Wi' lichtit e'e:
But wha the lassie is
   He ne'er lats dab!
O, fine I ken your state,
   My fykey Rab!
Weel, weel, it bude tae come
   I' the green o' the leaf.
An auld tale Granny hears
   Altho' she's deif!

CAENLOCHAN

I saw a herd of the wild red deer
In dark Caenlochan Glen.
They scented me, saw me, wheeled and fled,
Splashed through the burn, and upward sped
Into the mists on Monega's head,
And all that was left me then
Was an echoing splash in my startled ear
And a dream that beauty had been near;
Stag, and fawn, and following hind
Vanished and trackless as the wind;
Half a hundred wild things gone—
And dark Caenlochan left alone.

Once, on a long-time vanished night
You opened your mind to me.
Enchanted I looked. One fated word,
Clumsy, not false, I spoke. No herd
Of deer e'er fled so fast, or bird
Sprang from a shaken tree.
So fled your thoughts in panic flight,
Their fastness shrouded from my sight—
The proud, the tender ones, the shy,
Whither no friend or foe might pry;
And beauty glimpsed was swift withdrawn
As startled stag and soft-eyed fawn.

DUNSYRE

Red are the roads about the hills of Dunsyre,
　　And the soft spring rain is falling,
And circling slowly above the grass-green hills
　　The lonely whaups are calling.

The red road stretches between the emerald fields,
　　Where the little lambs are crying,
And over the wood in its purple flush of spring
　　The grey wood-doves are flying.

The plaintive keen of the golden plover haunts
　　My heart with its note so eerie.
The Black Mount towers above the soaking fields
　　In gloomy grandeur dreary.

Alone I walk on the red roads of Dunsyre,
　　Yet not alone I am walking,
For here in the rain, where the whaup and the plover mourn,
　　My grief is with me stalking.

"IN THE SPRING ———"

I've made the taps and the handles gleam
   Brighter than ever before;
I've scoured the paint and the bath with vim,
   And scrubbed the linoleum floor.
I've polished the set of mahogany chairs
   Till my arms are tired and aching;
With laying the carpet on the stairs
   My back is nearly breaking.

I've dug the whole of the kitchen rows
   And planted the lettuce and beans;
Excepting myself there's no one knows
   What this frenzy of energy means,
I'm trying to work you out of my blood,
   And out of my heart and head;
But you're blazing there in the brass and wood,
   And alive in the lettuce bed.

MOLLY'S SONG

Och! the joy o' thinkin' that yourself would be a-wooin' me!
The agony o' fearin' ye may think I am pursuin' ye!
The interest o' standin' by, to see what will I do wid ye!
   Och! but I'm tormented wid the storrum in me heart!

You're the boy would tantalise a girl wid the eyes o' ye,
Lookin' straight an' steady the unspoken things that lies in ye,
Searchin' wid their deeps o' blue the foolish and the wise o' me,
   Och! but I'm demented wid the storrum in me heart!

Sorra tak' the day I first began to feel the pull o' ye!
Sure it's Love the divil that has made a foolish tool o' me!
Me, that was as free as wind, and now me thoughts are full o' ye!
   Och! ye have me moidhered wid the storrum in me heart!

A PARADOX

Fate separated us, and you
Who were already dear, grew dearer.
You have come back, and strange but true
When you were distant, you were nearer.

DESTINY

"I will not see too much of her," said he,
"Because I fear
Lest this sweet woman grows too dear,
And I would still be free."

"I will not think too much of him," she said,
"Love's chains, tho' gold
"Too binding fetters make, I hold.
I do not choose to wed."

But in the stars their destined children sang,
"Our time will come!"
Amid the laughter and the hum
Their happy voices rang.

THE VAGABOND

All along the highway, the winding luring highway,
    A vagabond is singing like the Miller o' the Dee,
"I care not a farthing, a single brass farthing,
    For anyone I ever met, and none cares for me!"

"O, the jolly freedom, the lighthearted freedom,
    My partners the stars and the road!" sang he,
"And none to deny me the great broad highway,
    Whereon to adventure, alone, carefree!"

Listen to the blackbird, the jolly whistling blackbird,
    He sings to the mother-bird that sits on the nest.
"O, get you home, you vagabond, your wandering allures you,
    But little ones to greet you, and a wife to love are best!"

TO A GENIUS

You are too great for me. I cannot follow
Your spirit in its eager, upward flight.
Your thoughts race past me swifter than the swallow,
Or like the lark, they soar beyond my sight;
Or startling as a brilliant arrow cleaving
The quiet evening dusk above a stream
You flash, an ecstasy beyond believing,
Kingfisher-like, elusive as a dream.

Fain would I be the clay that housed the swallow
When home he darted in the twilight grey;
Fain would I be the humble grassy hollow
Where nests the singing lark at close of day;
Fain would I be, one moment of delight,
The pool whose mirror caught the sapphire flight.

THE GOLDEN EAGLE

My life is still and clear, and cool,
    Unstirred by wind, unrocked by tide:
A little green-encircled pool
    Where tiny weeds and minnows hide
    And distant stars reflected ride.

But once, upon a day of days,
    A golden eagle, soaring high
Came swooping out of noontide's blaze
    To drink my waters thirstily,
    And now is none so proud as I.

A PRAYER

Oh, Thou who dost forbear
   To grant me motherhood,
Grant that my brow may wear
   Beneath its maiden snood
Love to distressed Mankind,
   And helpful sympathy
For all whom Fate doth bind
   In Sorrow's company.

Help me always to choose,
   To comfort and to bless,
And in Man's service lose
   My fruitful barrenness;
So that my children may
   Succour and pity give
To sadder hearts, I pray
   Oh help me so to live.

STORM

The rain an' hail are tearin' on
Wi' fearsome din an' dash,
The very bed I lie upon
Dirls an' the snibbit sash
Lats in the winds that howl an' hoot
In keyhole and in lum:
This nicht the deil is surely oot
Wi' wild unholy drum.

I hap the blankets owre my face,
My hert it dirls wi' dread;
An' cowerin' doon amang the claes
Upon my maidenbed
I wish I had twa lovin' airms
To haud me ticht an' pet me,
An' ane to say "Ye're safe frae hairms,
The wild wind canna get ye!"

There's forces waur than winter's wrath
That fecht an' rive aboot me,
An' tho I try to keep the path
I aften sair misdoot me;
For whiles the winds come tearin' by,
Their on-dings fair beset me,
An' whiles I think I hear them cry,
"We'll get ye yet, we'll get ye!"

THE PRICE O' JOHNNY

"Oh, what's the price o' Love?" I said,
    A-counting out my money.
Old Life the Salesman shook his head.
    "'Twill cost a deal, my honey!
Have none o' it," he said to me,
"You're better far to keep your fee,
    And think no more o' Johnny."

"Nay, but I must have Love!" I cried,
    "While yet my cheeks are bonny."
Old Life the Salesman sadly sighed,
    A-picking up my money.
My peace, my sleep, he took from me,
Down to the very last bawbee,
    To pay for love o' Johnny.

My cheeks that were sae rosy-red
    Are paler noo than ony.
The joy I used to ha'e is fled,
    And cares are mony, mony.
'Twas true, what Life the Salesman spoke,
I bocht a dear pig-in-a-poke
    When I bocht love o' Johnny!

FAUSE FRIEND

Ye're dooble-jinted, soople-sawled,
An' slithery as an eel,
There's nane can lippen tae your word,
Ye twa-faced deil.

But wait, my birkie cheat-the-wud,
Ye'll no' aye jouk the lawin,
There's ane will mak' ye keep your pact
Some punctual dawin.

Ye've riped the pirlie mony's the time
Withooten ony skaith;
There's ane will tak' your measure yet
As sure as Daith.

LEEBIE SINGS

The geans in a' the glen are reid,
   And a' the willows weepin',
And a' the hives at Corrieheid
   And Dalnaclune are sleepin'.
The stags are roarin' ilka nicht,
   The winter's on us early,
But I am cheery aye and bricht—
   For sune I'll wed wi' Cherlie!

My Cherlie is a shepherd lad
   Abune the Linns o' Reekin,
He is the only lad I've had,
   And a' I'm ever seekin'.
And Leebie is his only lass,
   And oh! she loves him dearly!
Oh, haste ye, winter days, to pass—
   In spring I wed wi' Cherlie!

SPRING GANGS BY ME . . . .

The gairy-bee gangs by me
Bummin' wi' the news,
Pollen o' the catkins
Yalla on his trews.
The cordial o' springtime
Wiles him frae his byke
To feast amang the willow-saughs
By the rushin' syke.

The gowden-feathered coltsfoot
Brave amang the stour,
The bonny-scentit crimson
O' the curran' flooer,
The blackbird i' the lilac
Singin' matin'-fain . . .
But neither sang nor sunshine
My wound o' luve can sain.

THE WISHIN' WELL

A lass cam' sabbin'
    Tae my brink,
Tae dip her hand
    An' wishin', drink.
"O, water, water,
    Gi'e tae me
This wish I wish,
    Or else I dee!"

Back cam' the lass
    Years efter-hand,
An' peered again
    At my dancin' sand.
"I mind," she said
    "O' drinkin' here,
But—Losh keep me,
    What *did* I speir?"

HERESY

Turn the key
And seal the lock.
Let who will
Come by and knock.
Let him knock
And go away.
Call "No thank you,
Not today".
Call "No thank you"
But beware,
And to open
Never dare.
There is one
Who will pretend
He is come
To be your friend.
He will whisper
"Open wide
So that Love
May come inside."
Lock the door
And hide the key.
Keep your heart
In secrecy,
For he has
Another name.
Love and Sorrow
Are the same.

LISTENING

Spring again—
　But nevermore
His fingers tapping
　At my door.

Yet shall I
　Unsummoned know
Where his quick'ning
　Footsteps go.

Hear him pipe,
　And waken song
All the woodland
　Ways along,

And rejoice
　To hear his flute
Lead his choir,
　Tho' I be mute.

THERE WAS A SANG

There was a sang
That aye I wad be singin';
There was a star,
An' clear it used tae shine;
An' liltin' in the starlicht
Thro' the shadows
I gaed lang syne.

There was a sang;
But noo, I canna mind it.
There was a star;
But noo it disna shine.
There was a luve that led me
Thro' the shadows—
And it *was* mine.

64

SAE LANG HAS SORROW

Sae lang has Sorrow tenanted
The hoose o' Life wi' me,
An saut-like seasoned ilka meal
Wi' sharpened ecstasie,
That gin she cam' tae say Fareweel,
An' Joy hersel' cam' ben,
I doobt I wadna welcome her,
The bonny smilin' quean.

And at the lanely hinderend
Gin I sud tak' the road
Tae regions yont the yett o' Daith,
A sorrowless abode,
I doobt I wadna feel at hame
Sans sorrow an' sans sin,
But fleein' frae the wersh-like place
I'd tirl *anither* pin.

FATE

(from an old fable)

Fate fell upon a man,
Beat him
Well nigh to death.
And as she paused for breath
"Why thus assault me?"
The poor fellow said.

Dealing the wretch
A yet more grievous blow
Upon the head,
"Now that you ask me
Why, damme if I know
Myself" Fate said.

OVERDUE

O ragin' wind
An' cruel sea,
Ye put the fear
O' daith on me.
I canna sleep,
I canna pray,
But prowl aboot
The docks a' day,
An' pu' my plaid
Aboot me ticht,
"Nae news yet, mistress!"—
Ae mair nicht!

THE STRANGER

I met a man when I was drinkin' ale,
Wha yammered like a bird at break o' day.
But tho' his tongue was licht wi' joke an' tale,
His een were wae.

"Ye're whistlin' in the dark, my lad, that's plain,
Tae keep your spunk up," thinks I tae mysel'.
But what his trouble was I'll never ken—
The deid ne'er tell.

TOKENS THREE

Three things ye left ahint ye, lad,
　　The nicht I loot ye in,
A silken neckerchief o' blue
　　An' white, a silver pin.

The jewel in the pin, lad
　　It winked wi' yellow ee,
When in the cruisie licht, lad,
　　Ye crept anowre by me.

The cruisie licht was low, lad,
　　When saftly ye withdrew,
An' still we clung an' kissed, lad,
　　Wi' ne'er a thocht o' rue.

But neither neckerchief o' silk
　　Nor clasp o' cairngorm
Will haud or bind your word, lad,
　　Or hap me frae the storm,

Or hap me frae the storm, lad,
　　That braks aboot my heid
When ye'll be far awa', lad,
　　And I wi' springin' seed.

GIFTS

Clove carnations, pears,
Honey, a nectarine,
A tall Italian flask
Clear and water-green,
A pot of flowering heath,
A pearl, a piece of lace;
These have you brought to me
Love's lack to efface.

　　.　　.　　.　　.　　.

Bitter the honeycomb
Upon my bread,
Bitter your kindness, dear,
Now love is fled.

COMFORT IN PUIRTITH

The man that mates wi' Poverty
   An' clasps her tae his banes,
Will faither lean and lively thochts,
   A host o' eident weans—
But wow! they'll warstle tae the fore
   Wi' hunger-sharpit brains!

But he that lies wi' creeshy W'alth
   Will breed a pudden thrang,
Owre cosh tae ken their foziness,
   Owre bien tae mak' a sang—
A routh o' donnert feckless fules
   Wha dinna coont a dang!

"THUS I . . BUT LO, ME!"

Before me now ideals pass
   I fain had made my own;
But Time stands with relentless glass
Before me. Now ideals pass
Beneath his scythe. Like summer grass
   The hopes of youth are mown
Before me now. Ideals pass
   I fain had made my own.

Title from "The Temporary, the All,"
by Thomas Hardy.

WATER-OUZEL

(Cinclus aquaticus)

He keeps to the chosen stretch of his native burn,
Zig-zagging, if it does, close to its shining surface,
Alighting from time to time on his favourite stones,
Singing and trilling, the picture of sweet content.
Faithful he is to his white-limed perching places,
Bowing and becking and bobbing from right to left.
His white breast gleams on his black and russet shape, as
He sings and trills his water-accompanied song.

Anon, he wades in the shallows, and even, at times
He'll walk right under the water, or swim with his wings,
Searching for larvae and other aquatic creatures,
To feed his young in their high-domed mossy nest
With its little door on the floor, in the bank of the stream;
Or, as once I saw, on the parapet of a bridge,
High over the infant Clyde.

But best I remember the water-ouzel I watched
All of a summer day, in far Glen Lee;
Enchanted, I hid in the heather behind a rock
And saw my dipper fly through the vertical splash
Of the Falls of Unich, emerging to sing again
And bob on his whitened stone below the Falls.

Often, often, in later years, when harassed by the welter
Of modern life, the trappings of civilization,
I recall the ouzel's charm of song, the ripple of water,
The bird's devotion to his own particular stream,
(As mine to the Esk) and I tackle again my desk of duties,
And am refreshed.

VOICES FROM THE WATERSIDE

There's hazel, sauch and rowan
   Alang the braes o' Esk,
An' birks an' fir an' larches
Whaur bairns are at their desk.
The bogs are sweet wi' myrtle,
An' white wi' cotton grass,
There's whaup and peewit cryin'
Whaur moorland breezes pass.

     Pee-weet, pee-weet, pee-weet!

The coltsfit brings the springtime,
The rose, the month o' June
When cuckoo wi' his twa notes
Begins to change his tune.
The blackbird and the mavis
Sing heich abune their nest,
The rumlin river waters
Chirm on an' never rest.

     Cuckoo, cuckoo, cuckoo!

The swallows fish for insects
Heich in the caller air,
The bobbin water-ousels
Turn shingles for their fare.
The water-hennies chirrick
An' jerk 'mang beds o' reed,
An' hoddin' in the tree-taps
The croodlin' cushies plead.

     Coo-coo-cooo-c-cooo-roo!

The day wears on to gloamin'
An' river voices deepen,
The gorlins in their mossy nests
Are quaet noo an' sleepin',
The wuds are deep in mystery
An' when the dark comes doon
Ye'll hear the hoolets 'whooin'
Tae ithers neath the moon.

Hoo-hoo-hoo-hooo!

The Esk rins in oor memory
Early or late,
Siller in the simmer time
Peat gowden in the spate.
The Esk will find its ocean,
An' Life will find its fee.
We'll mind upon the Waterside,
Whaurever we may be.

Footnote:— Verses were spoken by individual children at Waterside School Glenesk, who imitated each bird-voice.

      After the final verse, all bird-calls merged together in chorus, then died out gradually, until only two owls remained, answering each other more and more faintly from a distance.

      This one-teacher school is now closed.

PORTRAIT OF A MATRON

Smooth and hard and cold to the touch are you,
A frost-cold apple hung on an autumn tree;
Acid-sharp and wholesome through and through
In your calm maturity.

May of the blush-pink blossom time must pass,
Spring and romance and fluting birds at play,
Petals falling on bluebells in the grass,
And summer floating away.

Wind and sun and dew have shaped your life,
Sharpened your sweetness, made you coldly wise,
Tinctured your satin beauty, a faithful wife,
With the glitter of frost in your eyes.

AN UNCO SICHT

The tragedy o' eld
Is no' to feel cauld,
But to feel the flicht
O' luve loup bricht
In a lamp that's auld.

Sae smoor yersel', my man,
Pit oot yer licht,
Grey hair that's tow
To a lassie's lowe
Is an unco sicht.

FOR AN INVALID CHILD

Cotton-grass down
    To pillow your head,
Milkwort-blue
    On your sprigged bedspread,
Fuchsia lanterns
    To guard your night,
And iris torches
    Golden bright.

Whispering pines
    And drowsy bees
To lull your pain
    With lullabies,
The Well of the Saints
    And hidden streams
To thread with silver
    Your darkest dreams.

The morning sun
    To touch your cheek,
The small bluetit
    Your sill to seek,
The breeze to chase
Your headache away;
And so, *"Yes, thank you,
    Better to-day."*

RAIN AND BIRDSONG

A raindrop in
A lupin leaf
May lift away
A load of grief.
A willow-warbler's
Ghost of song
May cut a sorrow's
Binding thong.
A primrose in
A lonely wood
May cool an anger
In the blood.

For man's inventions,
Speed, and noise
Are fretful pleasures,
Tiring toys;
But Nature's simple
Remedies
Are rain, and birdsong,
Silences.

A TEST

If, where the beech leaves thickly lie
  In golden autumn weather,
You walk sedately, stepping high
  Lest you should dim shoe-leather;
Or if you pass an orchard wall
  Where apples red invite you,
And never hear the tempter's call
  To steal 'just one' incite you;
Or if you bridge a country stream,
  Nor lean to look and wonder
If shadowy trout with scaly gleam
  Are quivering thereunder;
Or if you hear the night-owl's cry
  The woods with echoes filling,
And feel no sense of mystery
  Within your bosom thrilling;
Then, by these faded leaves of gold,
  Ripe fruit, chill waters falling,
You'll know, poor heart, that you are old,
  And owls your dirge are calling.

CAWS AND CAUCUSES

I

In elm-trees nou the craws are thrang
    Wi' gab and bicker up abune,
But eident to their darg they gang
In elm-trees. Nou the craws are thrang
And fine I thole their raucous sang
    For timely aa their biggin's dune
In elm-trees nou. The craws are thrang
    Wi' gab and bicker up abune.

II

In congresses the chosen gang
    Wi' gab and bicker never dune.
Hech! sic a sair aff-pittin' thrang
In congresses! The chosen gang
Will ne'er agree to psalm or sang,
    Or whilk precentor caas the tune
In congresses. The chosen gang
    Wi' gab and bicker never dune.

SONG OF THE SHEPHERD OF GRULINE

ISLAND OF EIGG

Long the winter stretched into spring,
Spring so bitter, and April cold.
Soft came May with her showers so warming,
Tender shoots in the hill grass forming.
    Ho ro Allival, Ho ro O!
    Ho ro Allival, Ho ro O!
Soft came May with her showers so warming,
    Ho ro Allival, Allival, O!

New grass came in a single night,
Filled the udders of ewes with milk;
Soft rain falling, and soft winds blowing,
Good the lambing, the ewes' milk flowing.
    Ho ro Allival, Ho ro O!
    Ho ro Allival, Ho ro O!
Soft rain falling, and soft winds blowing,
    Ho ro Allival, Allival, O!

Now the shearing is well begun,
Fleeces heavy, and flocks are fine.
Thanks to May and her gentle weather,
Kind to master and flocks together.
    Ho ro Allival, Ho ro O!
    Ho ro Allival, Ho ro O!
Thanks to May and her gentle weather,
    Ho ro Allival, Allival, O!

Tune: The Island Herdmaid

HOMESPUN

I met a man in Harris tweed
As I went down the Strand;
I turned and followed like a dog
That breath of hill and sea and bog
That clung about the crotal brown.
And suddenly, in London Town
I heard again the Gaelic speech,
The scrunch of keel on shingly beach;
The traffic's never-ending roar
Came plangent from a shining shore;
I saw the little lochs where lie
The lilies, white as ivory;
And tumbling down the rocky hills
Came scores of little foaming rills.
I saw the crofter bait his line,
The children herding yellow kine,
The barefoot woman with her creel,
The washing-pot, the spinning-wheel,
The mounds thrown up by patient toil
To coax the corn from barren soil.
With buoyant step I went along
Whistling a Hebridean song
That Ian Og of Taransay
Sang to me one enchanted day.
I was a man renewed indeed
Because I smelt that Harris tweed
As I went down the Strand.

"By permission of Punch."

IN THE NUNNERY GARDEN: IONA

Within this cloistered fabric, old and grey,
Roofless, turf-floored, with arches incomplete,
Spring from the broken walls and crevices
    Colour and fragrance sweet.

Plumes of valerian, crimson, pink and white.
Spires of blue lupin, blue as Chalbha seas,
Great scarlet poppyheads, and columbine,
    And gentle-eyed heartsease.

Rosemary, lavender, the sharp sweetbriar,
Clusters of wallflower, tawny-red and gold,
Shy little rockplants in their granite beds
    Groping to find a hold.

So may your House of Life, as years increase,
Harbour bright graces tho' the walls decay:
Courage and faith, tenacious as these flowers
    And beautiful as they.

MILKING TIME, BARRA

Seals are swimming mid the tangle,
Stretching up to look at Morag
As she sings upon the machair,
Kneeling by her milking pail.

Clear and green the tumbling waters
When the setting sun shines through them,
Through the breakers ere they tumble
Creamy white upon the shore.

Sweet the machair in the evening,
Yellow with the yellow crowfoot,
Creamy white with foam of daisies
Where the tethered cattle are.

Foam of milk within the cogan,
Foam of daisies on the machair,
Foam of restless breaking waters
While the kneeling Morag sings.

LILY LOCHS: HARRIS

Lilies
Ivory white on
Bronze and green
Float on the amber
Waters of lochans
Lone.
Are they gleaming nipples of nymphs unseen,
Lost Ophelias man shall never own?

Evening
Seals with silver
Their beauty rare,
Rooted deep in the silt
Of a thousand
Years.
Only the bending reeds in the moonlight fair
Whisper of secrets seen; but no one hears.

I HAVE SEEN FLAME FLOWERS

I have seen flame flowers in a lonely wood
In the Inner Hebrides,
Spire around stems of pine, and climb the air
To drip in scarlet from the sombre trees.

I have seen knolls where fairy queens of eld
Must surely dance and sport;
For royal purple, flecked with pink and mauve
Of thousand orchises adorned the court.

I have seen brackens on a headland steep
Above the breakers' flow,
Beneath whose frondy shade in summer heat,
Blue as the Cuillen, secret bluebells glow.

I have seen wreaths of snow in hot July
Pierced by the iris green,
For so the dazzling sands of Arisaig
Deceive the unwary traveller with their sheen.

I have seen rifts of rock so starred and gemmed
With saxifrage and thrift,
That neither Orient pearls nor rubies rare
From Scotland's loveliness my love can lift.

BALLAD OF A LOST LADYE

O Siller, siller shone the mune
An' quaiet swang the door,
An' eerie skraighed the flaughtered gulls
As she gaed by the shore.

O saft tae her the meadow girse,
But set wi' rock the hill,
An' scored wi' bluid her ladye feet
Or she cam' the place intill.

The sheen o' steel was in her hand,
The sheen o' stars in her een,
An' she wad open the fairy hill
An' she wad lat oot the queen.

*　　*　　*

There cam' a shepherd owre the hill
When day began tae daw;
And is this noo a seggit ewe
Or flourish frae the schaw?

It wasna lamb nor seggit ewe
Nor flourish frae the schaw.
It was the ladye bright an' still,
But she had won awa'

The peace an' loveliness upon
Her broo said, *"Lat abee,
Here fand I that I sairly socht,
Ye needna peety me!"*

LAMENT FOR SOLITUDE

The spirit of the Mountains
   Is weeping in the North,
That in the name of progress
   The fiat has gone forth
To rend and tear her strongholds
   And harness waters wild,
And drive out from her homeland
   Her dearest, dark-browed child.
   O weep, ye solemn fastnesses,
   Mourn, moor and loch and glen,
   For Solitude is gone, is gone,
   And will not come again!

O where will she find refuge
   Who knew the eagle's cries,
Where now men's noisy clamourings
   Re-echo to the skies?
What dirge will sing her rivers,
   Now doomed their course to leave?
What buried loves lie foundering
   Where prisoned waters grieve?
   She loved to linger brooding
   By lone rock-margined shore,
   But Solitude is gone, is gone,
   And will come back no more!

The spirit of the Mountains,
   She harboured sweet wild things,
And Solitude befriended them
   By secret pools and springs;
And in the starlit gloamings
   Bent many an antlered head,
But Fear the Stalker hunts them
   Now Solitude is fled.
   O where will peace find refuge
   Within the minds of men?
   For Solitude is gone, is gone,
   And will not come again!

AUTUMN COMPENSATIONS

Apples on the bending bough,
   Berries on the thorn,
Wheeling gulls behind the plough
   Where stood yellow corn.
Pungent petals, gold and white,
   Bronze and winey-red,
Blow in cottage gardens bright
   Tho' the rose is fled.

Books in cosy littered room,
   Feet in slippered ease,
Silver candles in the gloom,
   Stars in naked trees,
All the talks that daylight slew
   Shyly come again,
While we sit inside, we two,
   Cloistered from the rain.

We are growing old, my dear,
   Who were wild and young,
Wit informed and wisdom clear
   Fall now from your tongue.
Passion's perfume, beauty's flow'rs,
   May be past and dead,
But the mellow fruit is ours,
   Good as daily bread.

SCHIEHALLION

Years, long years ago, I read of a death I envied.
A girl climbing alone on this noble mountain
With its glittering quartzite cone,
Was caught in a thunderstorm,
Struck by lightning,
And killed.

She died, high up on the hill
In the lovely spring of her youth,
Under the lightning flash
With the boom of thunder
Echoing round and round.

The rain would be beating the sweet wild scents
From the honeyed heather,
The yellowy lady's-bedstraw, the creeping thyme,
And the tangy mountain grasses.

Rain-cleansed and sained by the scents
She died as quick as the lightning;
And I envied her a death,
So swift, so clean,
At the hand of heaven.

So would I die, thought I
As shortly after I climbed that self-same hill
(Young too, and happy and strong)
On a brilliant day of heat
That shimmered above the heather;
Far off, in the crystal air
Tummel and Rannoch lochs lay silver and blue,
(No pylons yet bestriding their virgin bounds)
And deep in the woods, the Lyon
Was leaping with salmon.
Fortingal slept by its ancient yew,
And windows eyebrowed with thatch.

And though I was happy and young
And hoped to climb many more Munros*
In my lovely Scotland,
I saw the prophetic years stretching ahead
When strength would fail and the weight of years
Would drag me down and restrict my urge
To climb to the top of the world.

Now, half a century on,
I lift my aching feet on the city stones.
My heart is heavy with thought of the
Hate in the world,
And the hideous problems wrought
By distrust and greed.
Is Prayer the Answer?

I think of the hills in their pure clean air,
And that man-made clouds of poison
May rest upon them, and us,
Annihilating all;
And I long to reach the crest
Of my earthly life, and gain
Schiehallion.

*Mountains over 3000 feet high

IDENTIFICATION

Your eyes were opened wide
When you came from your drowning:
Blue, so blue, and your lovely straight black brows
Were frowning.
And there was a little bruise—
The grappling hook, I suppose—
Or a stone, perhaps, had hit your brow
When desperate, you went under
With your coils of raven hair,
Still pinned so neat,
And your cheeks, so smooth and sweet
Now bleached, that were lovely
Couleur de rose.

You looked like a waxen doll on that narrow slab
When they drew the sheet.
"Yes," I said, unweeping, a frozen "Yes"
And I turned away,
Baffled, as never in life, by your blue blue eyes
That now had nothing to say.
I used to read so much in your eyes . . .
The water dripped from your crimson dress
And the little pointed feet
That were outlined under the sheet . . . .

EALASAID

Here are the shores you loved,
The tumbling waters,
Curdling and foaming on Atlantic strands,
The ocean, gentian-blue beyond believing,
The clean white sands.

And here the ancient speech
You loved essaying,
Rising and falling like the wave-borne birds,
The cadences that wind and tide are weaving
Of Gaelic words.

And here the little crofts
With thatch stone-weighted,
You told me of, so often ere I came.
How strange, that I am here without you, grieving
Your loved, lost name.

O fairest, loveliest,
Of Tiree's daughters,
White sea-bird, frightened in the city smoke,
Of all you loved the most, Life seemed bereaving
You; and your heart broke.

O, sleep you soundly now,
Ealasaid darling,
Beneath the sandy turf on Tiree's shore.
No more your island home you need be leaving,
Be sad no more!

FLOATING PETALS

"We love the cherry blossom, snowy white,
But it must leave the twig, and fall, and die,
And only some will fruit in colour bright,
And live again. For this is destiny."
So wrote Yoneko, of our loveliest,
Whose petals fell, and floated, and were lost—
All troubling thoughts deep-hidden in her breast,
No word for us, of what untimely frost
Scattered her blossom on death's lonely lake.
How many nights of questioning have I
Lain, desolate, and tearfully awake
With thoughts of her, and ever, why, and why?
Now comes this quiet message from Japan,
And even the fatal lake slips into plan.

PHOENIX

The channerin' worm doth chide, indeed,
That it hath lost its meat.
Nae sons sall lat me into yirth
Standin' at heid an' feet.
Nae spaad sall delve the bonny girse
Nor shear the gowans thro',
Nor habberin' buddies slaver roon',
Nor sexton dicht his broo;

But cleanly fire sall lick his lips
Whan this auld ane gangs hame,
An' flocks o' bonny feathered birds
Fluther aboot in flame.
Nae haet or rissom sall be fund
Whan Life has dune wi' me,
Till, Phoenix-like, I rise again
My Maker for to see.

NEAR TARFSIDE

A LANG GUIDNICHT

(Lang eftir Captain Alexander Montgomerie, 1545-1611)

Montgomerie, I rede thy solemn sang
   Quhen thou thy lang guidnicht fra luve hes tane,
That luve that fain thou wald hae keepit strang
   Wi thee ay thrang ere thou til erd had gane.
   Thou pled in vain. Alace, thy noble mane
Wes bot thy bane. Thou wes a seimlie sicht
Ontil that nicht quhen seikness hes thee slain
Deid clamed his awin, and thou did say 'guidnicht.'

Scotland, fra thy deir shoirs thy sons maun gae
   Quha fain wad stay gif they had bot the land
Quhair skeillie hand wald wark without allay
   By burn and brae to gar a hamesteid stand
   Siccar and sound, biggit on rock, nocht sand,
Or by some strand, shuve out the hameald keill
To fill the creill, keep aumrie ay weill fund
Wi bairns ay grand in happiness and heill.

Want ye the will, the wark to gar them bide
   By thine awin side, and thirl them til their hame?
Is't nocht thy shame, that they stend oceans wide,
   Oure deserts ride, or fremmit forests tame,
   Win deid or fame nocht til endow their name
Quhil uthers clame quhat suld be theirs by richt?
Is't nocht an uncouth sicht, thyself to lame,
Thy bodie maim, by bidding them 'guidnicht'?

Press Report. —45,000 Scots emigrated from Scotland in 1967.

LINES FOR WENDY WOOD'S SCOTTISH WATCH

Laughter and gibes and scorn
They brave for her:
Their pounds, their silver, and their pence
They give;
Their time, their talent and their youth for her
That she may live.

They love her hills, her streams,
Her "bridal falls,"
Her bones of rock, her peaks in snow
And mist;
Her barren moors, that should be gold again
With corn, sun-kissed.

They agonise in sordid
Tenements,
With children stabled worse than sheep
Or kye.
O, how can grace or peace or health abide
Such poverty?

They work to help the workless;
Start the looms;
To bring back colour, mirth to
Dreary streets;
To set the folk adancing in the glens
With light foot-beats.

We are the young. We know not
How to fear.
We will not tolerate these
Wasteful wrongs.
We will not rest, till Scotland rings again
With her children's songs.

DRY STANE DYKES

Oor forebears biggit weel withooten fyke
The cottar hoose, the byre, the drystane dyke.
Their horny hands were skeely, hard and strang,
Their life was simple, kennin richt frae wrang.

They helped a neebor fan the gudeman ailed,
At hairst or ploo, or fan the crops had failed:
Men o few words, but trusty freens in need,
Hard work their portion, an giff-gaff their creed.

Their gable wa's o biggins may be gane,
Dinged doon by bruckle brick, synthetic stane;
But roon the hills an haughs, the native kye
Still graze in peace in dyked security.

And lang may Scotland haud her ain traditions,
Yet claim her richtfu place in League o Nations.
Wha kens? Her wecht, the throwband stane micht be
Tae bind a shoogly warld in Amity.

(Throwband-stane: The long balancing stone thrust out on either side,
                   without which the dyke would fall, since it
                   contains no mortar)

WOMAN IN AUTUMN

Late bees trouble
The last of the clover,
Bare is the stubble,
Harvest is over.

Under my feet
The wild mint's breath is
Poignant, sweet,
As summer's death is.

Now by the park
For a moment linger,
Lips fruit dark,
And bramble-torn finger.

Ploughs are started,
Seagulls follow,
Where once darted
The dark-blue swallow.

The sharp blade tears
The stubborn field.
*What will next year's
Harvest yield?*

AUTUMN BERRIES

In spring o' life when charms were rife
   That are sae scanty noo,
The kisses o' my ain dear jo
   Were roses on my mou';
My he'rt was like a lintie singin'
On scentit sprays o' dogrose swingin'
   Wi' wine o' Maytime fu'.

But winter time an' sorrow's rime
   Ha'e driven my luve frae me,
An' frost has nipped my grace an' stripped
   The blossoms aff my tree;
But fruits o' knowledge burn fu' bricht
On the buss, tho' the bird lang syne took fricht
   That sang sae cheerily.

CORSTORPHINE WOODS

Ravens are kekklin' prophecies o' woe,
   Pyots in black an' white spiel superstitions,
The rooks mak' bedlam i' the elms below,
   An' saft-winged hoolets plan their midnicht missions.

Amang the haws an' brambles whinchats clink,
   The blue-tits flit amang their ferny covers,
The greedy gulls ahint the ploo-tail sink,
   An' hidden cushats croodle low like lovers.

Heich i' the frosty air, uneirdly cries
   Tell that a gaggle o' wild geese are flightin'—
Luik! there they are against the parchment skies,
   Like movin' brush o' ancient Chinese writin'.

Near hame, the ruif-heid raws o' stirlins haud
   Their evenin' guild o' scandal and o' chatter,
And sparrows, randy gossips, rogue or jaud,
   Scavenge their hindmost crumb wi' fuss an' clatter.

And, as I roond the corner, best of a',
   The mavis, singing on my gavel wa'—
Happy am I, altho' I bide my lane,
   To ha'e a singin' hert that's a' my ain.

SEA BUCKTHORN

Saut an' cruel winds tae shear it,
   Nichts o' haar an' rain—
Ye micht think the sallow buckthorn
   Ne'er a hairst could hain;
But amang the sea-bleached branches
   Ashen-grey as pain,
Thornset orange berries cluster
   Flamin', beauty-fain.

Daith an' dule will stab ye surely,
   Be ye man or wife,
Mony trauchles an' mischances
   In ilk weird are rife;
Bide the storm ye canna hinder,
   Mindin' through the strife,
Hoo the luntin' lowe o' beauty
   Lichts the grey o' life.

JEAN ARMOUR, FROM THE SHADES

The Januar wund is blawan cauld
   And aince again your name is ringan,
And still in spite o' Daddy Auld
   Ye've set aa Scotland singan.

I'm mindit on yon far-off e'en
   Whan first ye pit me in a swither
And on the snash cam' us atween
   Afore we bucklit richt thegither.

But aye it maittered nocht a blad
   What this ane said or that ane minted,
Ye were my ane and only lad
   Atween us luve was never stinted.

For tho' your fancy garred ye rove
   In airts whaur I cud never be,
I kent, dear Rab, your benmaist luve
   Wad aye come hame, come hame to me.

SONG OF PITY FOR REFUGEES

Snaw is bluffertin' the toun,
Gurly wunds are roustin' roun',
Peety fowk in broken shoon
   This winter nicht.

Peety help the weary auld,
Claes nor fire to fend aff cauld,
Hoose nor ha' them safe to hauld
   This winter nicht.

Peety wham in a' the warld
Fortune fell through hell has harled,
Hungert, hameless, broken, marled,
   This winter nicht.

Peety men withooten kin,
Ne'er a freend to cry them ben,
Nane their deein' sauls to sain
   This winter nicht.

THE BRACELET

No bracelet of bright hair about the bone
   Is emblem of my life's enduring passion,
But semi-precious gem or polished stone
   Declares my love of Scotland in my fashion.

Dowson and Donne, both fast in loving thrall
   Have left posterity immortal lines,
Much humbler I have but a simple tale
   Of symbols of true love in Scotland's stones;

The stones that nestle where the rocks abound
   On tide-washed beach, or in the river bed.
There nature leaves her treasures to be found,
   The silver-grey, the purple, gold and red.

Agate and onyx, crystal, chrysoprase,
   Garnet, cornelian, topaz, olivine,
Recall the search on wet or halcyon days
   By pebbly beach or lonely mountain stream;

Stippled and freckled things (by Hopkins praised)
   Banded with white and black, and red and green
Pounded by seas, by fellow stones abrased
   Until the lovely inner hues are seen.

And silvered o'er in memory's linking chain
   This pebble bracelet on my ageing wrist
Recalls the beauty of our ancient land,
   Of golden cairngorm, moonstone, amethyst.

PREDATORS

Behind the kiln, a quarry hole,
And in the hole deep water lies,
And in the water, water-weed,
With whitish flowers and loathsome flies;
And in and out the choking root,
The broken twig, the rusty can,
A slowly cruising presence lurks
As old as neolithic man.

A hundred years, they said, he'd lived,
When I, awe-stricken, rising three,
Clutched safety at my brother's hand
And peered, this cannibal to see.
So wicked and so huge he was,
Preying upon his fellow trout,
That everywhere he steered himself,
Dark terror circled him about.

Compound of greed, and lust, and power,
Secret and ruthless, keen to strike,
I know a man, I know a man,
I know a man, that's like a pike.

HALLOWEEN

Four times I have washed my dead for their final journey,
(Two for the kindly earth, and two for the fire)
And gracious memories live of my four dead kindred
(Two, in the heathery hill, and two in the pyre).
They all went, leaving mourning friends behind them:
Memories gay or sad, but sweet to recall;
But the fifth and finest, who haunts each living moment,
He is the one whom I loved best of all.
He is the one who lives for me this evening,
He whom I could not serve in death, nor claim.
He is the one who lives with me this evening,
The one I must not name.

AT THE END

Lay my body in fire when life is over,
Fire will I have for my swift and perfect lover.
My splendid body I will not have defiled
(O tender body that knew not lover or child)
By the slow and filthy lips of a crawling lust.
In one swift heat let me burn to a cleanly dust.

O swift and passionate, worshipping colour and heat,
Yet virgin-cold shall I come to my last retreat.
In terrible flame shall I savour at last my dream
Then ride the tempest, or drown in the raging stream,
And wheresoever my dust shall fall to earth
Some flower maybe will spring to a brighter birth.

But where this passionate self will go, God knows,
Who knows whence the lightning comes, and whither it goes.

WITCH-HAZEL

(Hamamelis Mollis)

I ken the Queen o' Candlemas,
Amang the snaw she stands,
Bare airms, an' cauld feet,
An' candles in her hands.

I ken the Queen o' Candlemas,
She disna mind the snaw,
She's the Queen o' witcherie
An' burns the cauld awa.

I ken the Queen o' Candlemas,
Frae far Cathay she comes,
To deck hersel wi gowden flooers
Tied up in silken thrums.

2 February, 1971

PERADVENTURE

Genesis XVIII: 32

Peradventure
Era
Rut
Advent
Dare
Venture
Even
Need
Ten
Under
Read
End.

NOTE.—The author had once hoped to found a
literary magazine, to be called "The Peradventure,"
if ten just men could be found to finance it. Alas!

EPISTLE FOR
CHRISTOPHER MURRAY GRIEVE
ON HIS 75TH BIRTHDAY

Dear Chris, dear Hugh, an dear-hoo-mony a name
Ye've used tae mate yer reengin thocht an word,
Ye've "kept the pottie boilin" this lang time
When younger makars cudna dree their dird,
Or else lost hert an howp, an owre short-windit,
Pit doon their pens, and "loot the cattie dee";
But na, ye ne'er gied in, tho fowk ill-mindit
Cried oot upon ye, thocht ye'd tak the gee.

Frae peeny-days thae bairn-lik phrases date,
Frae village playgrund or the Angus toun
Whaur ye begood the game o bein poet
An made a name weel-kent the haill warld roon—
But mebbe no i the Parish o Montrose,
Tho noo, nae doot, they're fidgin-fain tae claim
The young reporter-chiel, that neth the rose
Scrieved gowden lyrics that first brocht him fame.

Years efterhand, I mind in Edinbro
Colloguin owre some poet's toil-an-moilin
Ye said "It maitters no wha's writin noo
Sae lang's they keep the Scottish pottie boilin";
An years sin-syne, noo ye are seeventy-five
(And I sax years the mair) ye're eident makin
Yer poems spring as fresh, as still ye strive
Tae kep their glisk thro drumlie darkness brakin.

I never ettled, na, yer worth tae weigh
Nor yet tae set me up interpreter,
But frae Esk waterside, I've watched ye swey
This wey an that, whiles wild as Border river
That braks its bounds in spate, ca's doon a' fences,
Syne neist day comes sweet-purlin thro the braes,
Yet steers a coorse like "Ballad of Five Senses"
Frae whilk I wale thae lines, sae fu o grace.

106

"Oot o' the way, my senses five,
I ken a' you can tell,
Oot o' the way my thochts, for noo
I maun face God mysel."

And sae I name ye a *releegious* poet,
The foremaist ane frae John o' Groats tae Wamphray,
Agnostic? atheist? pagan? Deil a bit o't,
Chief pillydacus o' the haill clanjamphrie!
I mind o ane that bore in wind an weather
A sacred load thro cataracts o' thocht.
Na, CHRISTOPHER, yer faither an yer mither
They didna wale *that* wechty name for nocht.

FOR ONE IN TROUBLE IN SPRINGTIME

'I am the Necessary Angel of Earth'
—WALLACE STEVENS

I would have you look at growing hedges
To see the beads of green before they break,
Ebony blackthorn with its pearly silver
Making the lanes cobwebby with its lace.

I would have you watch the wanton sparrows
Flutter their wings in love's absurd conceits,
Proclaiming laggard spring is surely coming
Tho' snow-wreaths muffle still the dry-stane dykes.

I would have you look at furrowed ploughlands
Flashing with seagulls diving for their food,
The old eternal round that leads to harvest
When fields now bare will stand in golden stook.

I would have you listen in the evenings
To gaiety of Mozart, strains of Bach,
Knowing that complex fugues of stubborn problems
Will work out to perfection at the last.

I would have you rid your blood of toxins
Cleansing your mind of hurts, remote or near,
Pray that each day will be a new beginning,
So may you soon be well again, my dear.

AT A SANATORIUM

Her hands were clasped on the polyanthus bunch
Whose wrinkled leaves encircled the deep maroon
Of petals, laced with gold.

Evading the farewell purpose of my visit
I spoke of the cottage garden where I picked
The crimson velvet posy edged with gold,
Describing the gravel-paths, box-edged,
The appleringie and
The curling-stones at the door.

A glass on my desk had kept the flowers fresh
All day till I gave them into the wasted hands
That seemed all translucent bone;
And then, her fever meeting the dewy coolth,
A tiny cloud of vapour formed, and
Began to spiral upwards from her hands,
Until the hollow cheeks with their fatal flush
Were wreathed in quivering vapour, and
She wore an ethereal air as she bent
In saintlike adoration over the flowers,
Her bedrobe falling about her in
Mediaeval folds.

So I recall her, after these many years,
A wraith of miraculous spectral grace
Who now is only a graven name
On a stone at a little church in Cumberland.
"Isabel, aged twenty."

THE OLD FARMER

Locked in his deafness and his memories
He sits, unmindful, in the corner chair
Of all the gossip of the kitchen group
Who chatter cheerfully of this and that.
His hand unsullied now by farmyard toil
Strays kindly on the cat upon his knee,
And when some member of the family
Raises his voice to shout news in his ear
He smiles his gratitude, but then, alas,
Must shake his silvered head to indicate
That still he cannot hear; and so
Falls back again upon his memories.

Nights in the lamplit byre when calves were born,
The sheep dug out from snow drifts on the hill,
The harrowed field, the carted rounded stones
That long ago lay in the river bed,
Hours stolen from the farm to cast his line
Down at the waterside for speckled trout,
The sunrise walk to search his rabbit snares,
The weather watch to keep till corn was ripe,
The clipping time when neighbours rallied round.

The day his son was born to follow him,
The anxious waiting at the hospital
Years later, when his wife slow-dying lay:
That same year, too, old Bob, the farm horse fell
At his last ploughing, faithful gentle Bob,
He was a good one, but his time had come;
Best to forget the knacker's casual chat
And walk behind the stable with his dog,
To light his pipe until the float had gone.

The laughter rose and fell and teacups rattled
Around the kitchen fire.
                              He hears it not
But strokes the sleeping puss upon his lap,
Drinks up the proffered cup, and then it's time
To shuffle off to bed.

ONE ASPECT OF A POET

I sometimes think
That elusive bird, the Poet,
Is like the bower bird of the South
That adorns his territory with
Coloured scraps of salvage
Bottle tops, pebbles, rags of pyjama cloth,
And exotic petals of vivid hue—
Garnered from near and far;
Or our homelier blackbird
Weaving into his nest
Discarded bits of Cellophane,
A note thrown away by the milkman,
Or silver paper from a chocolate bar,
Along with native grass, and aubretia
Torn from the rockery;
Or the twinkling bluetit, using
Ravelled-out wool from a girl's jumper,
Or combings of hair—
Once in the Highlands, I saw
An exquisite nest in a niche of a bridge
Cosily lined with sheep-wool and deer-hair,
Where the tiny scrap of sizzling energy
Had built the cradle for his multiple brood:

So, from his magpie collection of
Facts and ideas,
Garnered, remembered, or
Filched from all quarters,
The poet fashions his lines.
And we, walking on earth-borne feet
Marvel at the grace and scope of his skill,
His soaring flight, his protean imagination,
And look and listen, indulgent,
As did Dylan's Milk Wood pastor
When naughty Polly Garter sang
As she scrubbed;
And like him we say
As we pause, then pass on,
Thank God for Song.

PRIMROSES FOR A BIRTHDAY

For Mary and Ian Munro

They brought primroses and anemones
From Hillside, near the village of my birth,
Delicate twigs of beech with moth-like leaves,
Green emblems of that dear remembered earth;
And childhood memories awoke again
Of crumpled leaf and candid yellow face,
Of purple speckled orchis, marigold
Garnered in Martin's Den or plashy place.
Often I wandered by my father's side
When he set out with fishing rod and reèl
To try the evening rise on Esk or Lade;
My goal to fill the basket, his, the creel.

One day I boasted in my Latin class
"My father caught four finnock in the Esk"
"With fly? What fly? What weight?" the teacher cried
And fidgetted, trout-haunted at his desk.
He taught us much besides our Latin verbs,
Softened our drudgery with nature lore,
Mixed *artifex* with flowers, trees and herbs
So that our Georgics never were a bore.

Back to the river and the Ponnage Pool
Where Colin Wood, my mother's father played
A fish* for nineteen hours, that "got away"
Later, found dead, it was named "Colin's spade."
A mile above the Pool there was a bank
Where much-sought-after quaking grasses tinkled.
We called them "shakky-trimlies," took them home
To our best vase where crystal pendants dangled
To grace the mantelpiece of "ben the hoose."
A lustre bowl of primroses would stand
On the round table in the window nook,
The horse-hair covered sofa near at hand.

* A report of this incident appeared in *The Montrose Standard* of November 8, 1866. The press cutting is now in the Folk Museum, Glenesk. The salmon's weight was estimated at 60 lbs.

How many years have flowed from Then till Now
Bearing their balanced freight of loss and gain,
And tho' I often long for Angus days
I've found much joy in my adopted town;
And chief of this has been the realm of gold
The poets offer to the questing mind.
In our old Makars' lines are treasures rare
Of language, art, of wit and thought profound:
Douglas, Dunbar, and Robert Henryson
And gentle Hume of *The Day Estivall,*
And many more too numerous to name
With Ramsay's *Evergreen* the best of all.

This path I followed, as I once had sought
Flowers in forests dusk, and plashy places
And later, Alpine plants on starker rocks;
So, sterner reading yielded further graces.
Then, by good luck I later came to know
Our living poets in their various fashion:
Spence, and Macgillivray the sculptor-poet
Proved different media shared common passion.
Soutar of Perth and Jeffrey from the West
(Both conquering pain by their creative art)
Have left a legacy for those who seek
To stretch the intellect and warm the heart.
And "Hamewith" too, I counted as a friend
Who from his exile in a southern clime
Employed his antique Doric, yet today
"Gin I was God" is relevant to our time.
What of the women? Violet of Dun
And Marion Angus, sib to Lady Nairne,
All laid their tribute at old Scotland's feet,
Like coloured stones upon a mountain cairn.

These now are gone to swell Dunbar's "Lament"
But leave their work behind for us to cherish.
Now others write to keep the Muse alive
Even in this age when worthy causes perish;
But peradventure ten just men are found
Hope bargains still to salve the writer's art
And younger bolder spirits soldier on
In brave experiment to play their part.

Thus have I pondered, when at age four-score
My younger author friends had come to meet me
At Ashgrove House, where food and wine galore,
Kindness and candles were laid on to greet me:
There Valda thrust primroses in my hand
Crying "These flowers came from Crowdieknowe,"
Bridging the lengthy saga of my years,
Both good and bad, flowing from Then till Now.
And I am rich, and rich, and rich indeed
(Let cynic say my spectacles are rosy)
To hoard a wealth of poems in my head
And span a lifetime with a primrose posy.

15 May 1966

ON BEING EIGHTY

Broad in the beam? More broad in sympathy.
Stiff in the joints? More flexible in mind.
Deaf on the right? Now voices from the Left
In politics and art more clearly sound.
Arteries harden? Movements then more slow
Allow more time to contemplate and ponder.
High on the Shelf? Horizons farther grow
Extending faculties for joy and wonder.
Acceptance gained of what one has to bear?
The hard is then become more bearable
And comrade Death himself finds welcome, so
Quite cheerfully towards eighty-one we go.

ELEGY FOR SUSIE

Two dimpled cheeks
That bracket grave young lips,
Eyes questioning
(The question with
No answers).
Fingers too frail
To grasp Life's nettle whole,
Feet faltering
Tho' shaped like ballet dancer's.

What can I say?
There are no words to tell
Why tears alone are left
Where should be
Laughter.
The tolling bell rings out.
Too young, too young,
Too young, too young,
She should have died hereafter.

18 January 1968

SPRING IN THE MEARNS

IN MEMORIAM, LEWIS GRASSIC GIBBON

Clouds of smoke on the hill
Where the whin is burning,
Staining the clear cold sky
As the sun goes down.
Brighter the fire leaps up
As night grows darker;
Wild and lovely the light
Of the flaming whin.

Blackened the stubborn bush;
No more the golden
Nut-sweet blossom shall lure
The wandering bee.
Twisted branches sink
To a sullen smoulder
Where the small stonechat clinked
Contentedly.

Come again, when the rains
Have carried the ashes
Into the hungry soil,
And lo, the green!
Earth that was seared by fire
Has now begotten
Tender herbage for tough,
Grain for whin.

Body of man to death,
Flesh to ashes,
Muscle and tissue and bone
To dust are come.
Ah, but the spirit leaps
From the cindered fibre,
Living, laughs at death,
That is but a name.

Life goes on for ever;
The body smoulders,
Dies in the heat of the pace,
Is laid in earth.
Life goes on; the spirit
Endures for ever,
Wresting from death itself
A brave new birth.

This man set the flame
Of his native genius
Under the cumbering whin
Of the untilled field;
Lit a fire in the Mearns
To illumine Scotland,
Clearing the sullen soil
For a richer yield.

Arbuthnott Churchyard, 23rd February 1935

LOVERS THREE

Came one
With laughter fleet,
Flashing eyes
And dancing feet,
Played the flute
So charmingly,
Set my heart
A-fire in me.

Came then
With sober face
One who frowned
On frolic grace,
Chanted sounding
Tragedy,
Thrilled the marrow
Bones of me.

Which then
Shall I take,
Joy or Sorrow
For my make?
While I pondered
Life passed,
Time revealed
My Love at last:

On my lips
A chilling breath,
In my ears
The voice of Death.
I resolve
All doubt.
I choose
You out.

VIRGIN SONG

Thy power so penetrated me,
    Thy mind so pierced my own
That I, who barren was of old
    Have to fruition grown;
And thoughts I have conceived of thee
    Shall make my spirit great
Altho' the utterance of them
    Come forth by sorrow's gate.

And tho' the body of my desire
    Grow lean for lack of thee,
And never, never shall I now
    Thy children's mother be,
This child of song thou givest me
    Shall tend my lonely years
Tho' yet 'tis but a stammering thing,
    A nurseling born in tears.

TACHYCARDIA

The bird in my breast
Is beating its wings
And willing its way
To be free.

O where will it go
On escaping the cage
Of my ribs,
O where will it flee?

O where will it flee
When body lets go
And spirit and mind
Are free?

Will it fall to the earth,
Or fly to the sky,
Or sink in the depths
Of the sea?

The bird in my breast
Is soon to be free,
For now, I
        can
            hardly
                  see,
I am NOT
        afraid
But I'd
      like
         to
            know
What
      now
         will
            happen
     To ME.

JOURNEYING

In youth I battled
With the elements,
Leaning against the wind,
And when it suddenly fell,
I fell with it.
Laughing, I picked myself up,
Ignoring bruises,
And merrily journeyed on.

In middle life,
Not Dante's dark wood,
But a rushing stream
Impeded me.
I crossed on stepping stones,
And when one turned
Under my foot,
I toppled into the stream.
Laughing I picked myself up
Shaking myself like a dog,
And gained dry land again.

Now, I journey
More slowly,
Grimacing sometimes
With pain, but
Plodding on,
Placing each foot
With care.
A broad stream
Looms ahead.
This I must cross.
Will the trumpets
Sound for me
On the other side?
Or shall I founder,
Mid stream,
And float with
Other flotsam
Out into the oblivious waters
Of the cold North Sea?

BUITS

She reeshled in the wudden kist
    I' the corner o the barn,
An fuish me oot my auld buits
    Weel-stappit frae a' harm.

The leather shone as guid as new
    Thae forty year or mair,
The taes were patcht, an tackets lost,
    But "Dod," I thocht, "they'll wear!"

I mindit on the mony miles
    The while I tied the laces,
Whaur thae auld buits had cairried me,
    Owre muirs an mountain faces.

They'd plowtered mony a rashy bog,
    For Flooers o' Parnassus,
An asphodel an butterwort
    Sundew an cotton-grasses.

Ben Nevis hicht they'd compassed richt
    A' Scotland spread afore us,
An thro Glencoe wi Nance for jo
    They'd h'ard us birl a chorus.

The Isle o' Mull they'd circled weel
    Frae Tob to Craiganure,
Ta'en in Iona on the road,
    An conquered great Ben More

They'd braved the Cuillin rocks o' Skye
    An slopped thro Sligachan mire,
They'd wandered singin sands o' Eigg
    An gowden Luskentyre.

Tae Heaval tap on Barra's Isle,
    They'd taen me wi great ease,
An scrambled owre the tangled rocks
    O Hebridean seas

Frae Tushielaw tae Langholm toun
    An Cheviot's Border valleys,
They'd taen the road the drovers trod
    Past scenes o reivers' rallies.

By Yorkshire dale and Pennine vale
    Helvellyn's Striding Edge,
They'd taen the track in wind and wrack
    By tarn and scree and sedge.

The Pentland Hills they aften trod
    Frae Kips tae Cauldstaneslap,
(But nivir solved the mystery o'
    The cap on Tintock Tap)

And owre and owre and owre again
    They'd tramped an Angus Glen,
By Isla, Clova, Prosen, Esk
    An owre tae Aiberdeen.

But aye the road they bude tae come
    And ane they airted maist
Was "up the Glen" tae Tarf and Esk
    The bonniest an the best.

An that's whaur they hae roostit noo,
    Weel-tendit in the kistie,
And WELCOME tae my auld buits
    Wae's me, but I hae missed ye!

An tho I'm past the auchty mark
    An traivel is a trauchle,
Fegs, wi thae buits upo my feet
    The Rowan Road I'll tackle.

An thanks tae a' the Parsonage fowk
    That follow Gladys' biddin,
She's fed me weel, restored my strength,
    An saved my buits frae the midden.

Written for Gladys Guthrie, Tarfside, June 1967.

123

THE WHITE HORSE

"Behold, a white horse, and he that sat thereon, called
Faithful and True" Revelations, 19—11.

The old white horse in Waggle's Field
    That drooped across the fence
Spelled "holidays" for all of us
    As we drove to the Glens.

We hailed him from our wagonette
    Drawn by our pair of horse,
(Hired from the stables of "The Star"
    In our home base of Montrose.)

We always looked for the sad old face
    Stark-white on the uphill field
And shouted greetings to his ears
    Altho' he paid no heed.

He was worn out with dragging cart
    And plough and stone-choked harrow,
So, pensioned off, he drooped and sagged,
    No work for his tomorrow.

"Too old for work" my father said,
    "A family pet" said Will.
We waved goodbye, and travelled on
    To reach the Rowan Hill.

Then came the year, he wasn't there
    "He must be dead" said Jim.
A cloud fell on our holiday,
    We shed a tear for him.

He never knew we valued him,
    We never knew his name,
But somehow future holidays
    Were never quite the same,

For doubts of growing-up set in,
    And even of growing-old,
The chill of not being quite-so-safe,
    What would our future hold?

I think of him as once he was
    With long white tail a-toss,
And flying hoof and silver mane,
    A very Pegasus.

Perhaps in some Elysian field
    Birk-scented, clover-sweet,
He grazes now, exempt from age,
    All limber-limbed and fleet.

No longer drooping o'er the fence
    But active, young and gay,
King of the stable, well-beloved
    Fed on the choicest hay.

But now, some eighty years have fled,
    The wagonette crew all gone,
And *Burd-alane, I still recall
    The white horse in the Glen.

I wonder why his image comes
    So often in my dreams?
This old white horse in Waggle's Field,
    I wonder what he means?

Is it because the Rider comes,
    His white steed drawing nigh,
The dread yet dear Apocalypse,
    The longed-for day I die?

*Burd-alane: the last member of a family.

125

THE YEARS

The years hae stown the gowd o my hair
   The sparkle o my ee
   The spring o my step,
   The straucht o my back,
And the far o my sicht frae me, said she,
   The far o my sicht frae me.

The years hae taen the life o my kin,
   The warmth o their companie;
   The bairns by my side
   That I never had,
And the man that gied them tae me, said she,
   The man that gied them tae me.

The years hae gien me the wunds o the warld,
   The harvest o memorie,
   The bitter and sweet,
   The tares and the wheat;
The savour o Life itsel, said she,
   The savour o Life for me.

The years hae gien me the gift o sang,
   Tho cuist in a minor key.
   My back is bent,
   And my life near spent,
But it winna lat me be, said she,
   It winna lat me be.

THE WEIRD WIFE

(This dialogue was suggested by a picture by James Giles)

Far are ye gaun, ye weird auld wife
  Wi yer cloke an yer willow wand?
I'm gaun tae the end o' a weary life,
  Tae a far an fremit land.

Fat wull ye fin as ye journey there
  An stummle owre stick an stane?
The length o my strength my weird tae bear
  As I journey a my lane.

Fat wull ye eat fan the hunger gripe
  Wull be gruppin ye sair ere lang?
The reid clood-berries an brambles ripe
  Wull slocken me as I gang.

An fat wull licht ye fan mirk comes on
  An the gloamin licht dees oot?
I'll seek the mune an I'll lay me doon
  Fan the hoolets begin tae hoot.

An fat wull ye dae fan the reid fox rins
  An snuffles aboot yer heid?
The fox is my brither, as weel he kens,
  I hae nae need for dreid.

An fat wull ye say fan yer braith gies oot
  Like a gutterin can'le flame?
I'll mind my mainners, I hae nae doot
  "Guid een tae ye, DAITH, I'm hame."